M000190425

PREACHING
WITH PURPOSE
AND PASSION

*The Greatest
Call on Earth*

LIFE IMPACT SERIES

FRANK DAMAZIO

CityChristianPublishing
www.CityChristianPublishing.com

PUBLISHED BY CITY CHRISTIAN PUBLISHING
9200 NE Fremont, Portland, Oregon 97220

City Christian Publishing is a ministry of City Bible Church and is dedicated to serving the local church and its leaders through the production and distribution of quality equipping resources. It is our prayer that these materials, proven in the context of the local church, will equip leaders in exalting the Lord and extending His kingdom.

For a free catalog of additional resources from City Christian Publishing, please call 1-800-777-6057 or visit our web site at www.CityChristianPublishing.com.

Preaching with Purpose and Passion

© Copyright 2006 by Frank Damazio

All Rights Reserved

ISBN: 1-59383-036-X

Cover design by DesignPoint, Inc.
Interior design and typeset by City Christian Publishing.

All Scripture quotations, unless otherwise indicated, are taken from *The Holy Bible, New International Version*, copyright 1973, 1978, 1984 by International Bible Society. Used by permission. All rights reserved.

First Edition, July 2006

Printed in the United States of America

Table of Contents

Introduction

Preaching is without a doubt one of the most fulfilling aspects of the leader's ministry and life. Preaching also has the potential to frustrate, discourage, and bewilder those who are involved with the preaching ministry. In this book I hope to encourage all preachers to a higher level of love and achievement in your preaching. My prayer is that you will receive a fresh anointing of the Holy Spirit upon your preaching that will be evidenced in a significant way.

You are called to preach. You are separated unto God for this special privilege. Your commitment to the researching of the Word of God and dedication to developing all the skills available to you will determine your level of preaching. God desires that you become the best possible preacher that you can become. God desires to restore your passion for preaching, repair your broken altar of prayer, help you shed excess emotional baggage, and help you return to your first gift of preaching.

Your authority to preach comes from your divine appointment of God. You are called; you are chosen; you are set apart for this ministry. Isaiah 61:1 says, *"The Spirit of the Lord GOD is upon Me, because the LORD has anointed Me to preach good tidings to the poor; He has sent Me to heal the brokenhearted, to proclaim liberty to the captives, and the opening of the prison to those who are bound."* God has poured His spirit upon you. Receive this promise and move ahead.

1 Timothy 2:7 says, *"for which I was appointed a preacher and an apostle—I am speaking the truth in Christ and not lying—a teacher of the Gentiles in faith and truth."* You are appointed! Preach the Word. Be ready in season and out of season. God desires to give you a preaching

capacity that will preach to new spiritual depth and practical range that you never had before.

Let us agree with Martin Lloyd Jones: "Preaching is something very difficult to define. It is certainly not a matter of rule or regulations. Preaching is something that one recognizes when one hears it. True preaching is God acting. It is not a man uttering words, it is God using him." Join with me as we become the vessels of God to pour out His golden oil.

Seasoned preachers as well as beginning preachers will greatly benefit from this material. You can learn how to become a better communicator, read your listeners, find the right illustrations, craft your words with more force, pace yourself, and finish strong. Enjoy as you read *Preaching with Purpose and Passion*.

THE TEST OF A PREACHER IS
THAT HIS CONGREGATION GOES
AWAY SAYING NOT, "WHAT A
LOVELY SERMON!" BUT
"I WILL DO SOMETHING."

— *Rev. Billy Graham*

Part 1

The 22 Laws of Preaching with Purpose and Passion

I am not writing this book as one who has arrived. The only sense of arrival I have is that after every sermon, I know that I'll try to do better the next time. That's the sense that most preachers have. We never quite perfect every aspect of preaching. When we get the outline right, the Holy Spirit doesn't show up. And when the Holy Spirit shows up and there is a powerful presence, we have no content. And when we get the content and the Holy Spirit on the same day, the worship leader takes all our time.

There are any number of unique and challenging elements that come into this whole experience of preaching. Some of you may have questioned your appointment to preach because of what you see as a lack of fruitfulness in preaching. We sometimes tend to equate church growth with good preaching, but you could be a great preacher and not have church growth.

Others question their appointment to preach after they've been criticized. No one enjoys criticism and most people don't handle it well. Even preachers occasionally have fleeting thoughts of getting even with their critics. Some may pray, "Lord, give my detractors everything they so richly deserve." But whether the criticism leveled against you is right or wrong, it should not be allowed to change your heart. If you harden your heart or become bitter or cynical as a result of criticism you've received, you have made a wrong choice.

The preacher and apostle Paul was criticized consistently for everything from his looks to his preaching style to his desire to not accept money for preaching. His critics even questioned his right to preach. But Paul never wavered, testifying repeatedly, "I am appointed a preacher and an apostle." Paul was given the appointment—the authority—to preach by God and was not swayed from that appointment by his critics.

My authority to preach exists not because people voted for me, nor because I went to Bible college, nor because I came up with an outline and decided to try preaching. My authority comes from the appointment of God. I believe in the gift God has given me and I believe when all else fails—people, me, circumstances, the church—I must have the confidence that I can say before God and all people: "I was appointed to do this. I was appointed by God to preach."

To be a preacher of purpose and passion, you must have confidence in your appointment by God and receive this calling as one of the greatest gifts that God can give any human being.

The following *22 Laws of Preaching with Purpose and Passion* are principles and strategies that I have learned and used over the past 35 years as an appointed preacher. I believe every preacher could benefit from these laws. Some of them may be applied differently depending on your ministry, your location, your church, your flock. But in trying to be fresh, real, sensitive, and Word-based in my preaching, these are the values I respect, the laws I use and try to live by. I pray they will benefit you as well.

✦ **I.** *The Law of Filling Your Own Well*

A leader's spiritual condition will be evident in his preaching. An empty spirit, an empty well, cannot be hidden behind a flurry of fast or pretty words. Preaching is impartation, not just communication. "Imparting" implies giving a part—in this case, a part of yourself. The leader must keep his own heart and spirit healthy, growing, and full of the goodness and passion of God in order to pass these things on to others.

When your well is not full, you preach from your lack and insecurities. You may apologize too much. You may say things you wish you had not said. When your well is empty, you may preach from your mind instead of your spirit. You may not feel the difference, but your church will, your friends will, and your family will. The connection with people's spirits will not be made. Mind speaks to mind and spirit speaks to spirit. When you are filled with the Holy Spirit and you speak out of that reservoir, people respond—even if your words are weak and your outline is illogical and your illustrations don't hit the target.

If you minister out of a full well, they'll drink. Why? <u>Preaching is a spiritual act.</u> It's not lecturing or public speaking. I have no desire to be a public speaker; what I love is to be a vessel for the holy oil of God. I love to see a well so filled with the right virtues and the right spirit that it spills out over the people and you can see them drinking in.

Nothing will keep a leader's well filled better than ⊙consistent⊙ devotional reading of the pure word of God, coupled with prayer from the heart that is a true communion with the Father. <u>Set aside a specific time and place for your daily devotional and one-on-one prayer appointment with God.</u> Make this meeting time as unbreakable as a dental appointment. Hold on to this connection to God and God's Word throughout your day. His praise will *continually* be in my mouth, David said (Ps. 34:1). <u>Let God dwell in you, not just come</u> <u>for guest visits</u>.

Your ministry should be a well of living water. The London minister Charles Spurgeon talked about preachers whose wells had old cans and dead cats in them. <u>Don't let your ministry become</u> <u>an empty well littered with refuse. Fill it up</u>.

✦ ## 2. *The Law of Loving Sinners*

<u>People will hear what you preach only after</u> <u>they feel that you care for them</u>. The preacher must have a positive and healthy attitude toward the people he affects with his words and actions. Preaching with sensitivity and love makes biblical truths manageable for believers.

Preaching God's word means preaching that homosexuality is sin, that premarital sex is sin, that cheating on your income taxes is sin. Not all people like to hear these things. But while the preacher must hate the sin, he must show love to, and open his heart to feel God's love for, the sin-

GIVE ME ONE HUNDRED PREACHERS
WHO FEAR NOTHING BUT SIN
AND DESIRE NOTHING BUT GOD,
AND I CARE NOT WHETHER THEY
BE CLERGYMEN OR LAYMEN, THEY
ALONE WILL SHAKE THE GATES OF
HELL AND SET UP THE KINGDOM
OF HEAVEN UPON EARTH.

*— John Wesley, 18th-century Anglican
preacher and theologian*

ners. You must love preaching truth but you also must love the people to whom you are preaching.

Some preachers love their preaching more than they love the people, and that can be sensed by the congregation. If you pastor in one place for a long time, you begin to know the people's problems and you can become calloused toward them. You may begin to question why you preach, since the people seem to continue dealing with the same problems, the same disobedience to the Word, over and over. Even if you start out loving the people, you may become discouraged by their lack of change. When your heart loses compassion for people, it affects your message. You must love people whether they change or not. Your mission is to preach the Word with love; God is in charge of changing the people.

✦ **3. *The Law of Appreciating the Seasons***

A preacher will experience various spiritual seasons that will affect his preaching. When long, unexpected dry periods occur, the preacher may become concerned that he has done something to quench the anointing or that God has withdrawn a measure of anointing without explanation. A preacher must learn how to use the seasons for his benefit. A dry season is an ideal time to settle in and nurture deeper roots and solidify his foundation following a season of growth. The seasons of victory or sorrow, growth or discouragement, stillness or fruitfulness, can all be used by the Holy Spirit to bring breadth and depth to the preacher and his preaching.

Preachers should not allow these seasons of discouragement or disappointment to affect their messages. You should preach the Word no matter what you are going through personally. You should preach the Word as if you are living every aspect of the victory, even though you might be in a valley or in a dry time. It's very difficult for the sheep to eat when the preacher is pouring out personal problems instead of organic, Bible-based food.

Only a few times in over three decades have I ever exposed my difficult seasons from the pulpit. Some of you may do that often, and maybe you're good at it and can get away with it. "I can't believe the financial problems we're having." "We have all these health difficulties." "My wife is having a crisis." "My kids have been going through one disaster after another." Maybe some people can relate to your problems. But I think if you preach about your difficulties too much, you eventually pay for it. People start wondering, "When is he going to get through these things?" Or they think, "If he's going through this, and he's a pastor, then my life is really going to be messed up." Or "If he's feeling down, and he's a pastor, I'm going to be destroyed."

If I am in a valley, I don't preach on valleys. If I'm experiencing a financial difficulty, I don't preach on finance. If I am in a prayer dry season, I don't preach on prayer dryness. I focus on preaching the Word. If I preach the Scripture, I forget about my season. It keeps me from sharing all of my personal life all the time. There is a time to share some of your personal life, and that will be covered later. But rather than using the difficult seasons as sermon topics, use them to focus on your personal growth and to strengthen your spiritual foundation.

✦ 4. *The Law of Abiding Anointing*

When preachers linger too long and too often outside their spiritual gifting and calling, their anointing may seem to decline. Administration, program management, people problems, excessive non-biblical reading, or energy-draining activities may quench the preacher's spirit. Inspiration may evaporate and preaching may seem like harder work than before. We must at these times guard our hearts and our spirits. While we should do what we can to reorder our priorities, preachers must also remember that inspiration resides within the Word, not in the leader.

We may all have times that we preach by faith in the word of God even when we don't feel the anointing power. Sometimes we may try to holler our way out of it, or act our way out of it, or prophesy our way out of it. We may try every way to feel the anointing, but it can't be found in feeling or emotion. It's in the spirit.

The great preacher Charles Spurgeon once delivered what he thought was a good sermon but then considered it a flop when only sixty people got saved from the thousands he preached to. He went home and fell on his face and asked God for forgiveness, saying, "God, that's the poorest sermon I've ever preached in my life. There was nothing. There was no feeling; there was no anointing." Then he got up and prepared a masterpiece sermon; worked on it all week, crafted every word, added his illustrations, fasted, and prayed. The next Sunday he preached one of the most marvelous messages he'd ever crafted. Nobody came to the altar. Not one person. He left that service, went to his office, fell on his face, and simply said, "I understand the lesson." It's not by mind. It's not by power. It's by my spirit, says the Lord.

Sometimes you do everything you know how to do and there's no response. Other times, God says, "I like that message; I'll use it." And God goes to work. The anointing does not abide in emotion; it abides in the Word of God. And when you preach that Word, things will start happening in people's lives that you cannot produce otherwise. That is the law of the anointing. The Spirit will be present and will influence people because it resides within the Word of God.

✦ **5. *The Law of a Well-Fed Feeder***

Studying for sermons does not necessarily produce a well-informed mind. You can be very knowledgeable in Bible study and know nothing about the world. It's important to read books, including secular books, that expose you to material that stretches the mind and enlarges the vocabulary. The reading of the word of God consistently in different translations will feed the spirit and the mind, as will reading theological books. I also read secular books, and I read books I don't understand—books that I admit are beyond me. But if I absorb even if a little of what they say, it stretches my thinking into new issues and areas that I hadn't considered before.

A preacher should be well-read and well-informed in many areas—business, entertainment, culture, technology, theology, regional, and world events—in order to reach people where they live. Preachers who seclude themselves in exclusively Christian environments and make no effort to keep abreast of world changes will lose a sense of how to communicate biblical lessons to contemporary listeners.

As in all areas, though, the preacher must maintain a balance. Excluding biblical teachings and kingdom truths and providing instead entirely contemporary "infotainment" messages is a far more dangerous trend than being unaware of worldly influences.

✦ 6. *The Law of Learning Before Teaching*

Truth and knowledge must be absorbed and understood by the preacher before it can be effectively transmitted to the people. The word must become incarnated, literally embodied by the preacher. A message that arises out of the inner life will touch the inner life of others. As the preacher matures in Christ, his or her message matures, and then the church matures.

We want people who can say, "My pastor feeds me. He speaks as a mouthpiece of God and I am being changed." A woman recently stopped me at a gathering. She said, "I just wanted to stop and tell you something. We've never met, but I've been in your church seven years." I said, "Well, I'm sorry." She said, "No, nothing to be sorry about. I just want you to know my husband and I have looked forward to coming to church every Sunday for seven years." That's a blessing to hear because some people say the opposite. She said, "Every time we come under the word you preach, something is adjusted in our lives. Every time. One Sunday, it will be my husband. Then it will be me. It will be the kids. Or we leave here saying, 'Whew, we got an answer on that.'"

That's not something a preacher can plan to do. That's the Holy Spirit. To preach from a message of the Holy Spirit to the people is different than crafting sermons. You can't craft the touch of the Spirit into your sermons.

The seed of the Word must be planted in you in order to grow and mature. There must be incarnation, not just instruction, intellectualism, or illustration. Inhale the breath of the spirit in research and exhale the preaching of the Word in spirit. Inhale in research, but don't hold your breath forever. Some people are good at inhaling all the information, but they don't know how to exhale it. Learn that it's that breath of life that

IT IS NOT FITTING, WHEN
ONE IS IN GOD'S SERVICE, TO
HAVE A GLOOMY FACE OR
A CHILLING LOOK.

— *St. Francis of Assisi*

will bring life to the people. Exhale the fresh life of the Word.

✦ **7.   *The Law of Recognizing Red Flags***

Beware of preaching from the pulpit to correct a specific problem, person, or activity in your church. Be wary also of preaching when you are feeling critical or unsettled about something going on in the church. Combining overall fatigue with either of these conditions should start red flags waving. When the preacher goes to the pulpit with upset emotions, a fatigued mind, and/or a dose of discouragement, he is very apt to say things he was not intending to say, or become overly emotional without reason, or have a condemning and harsh attitude. None of these, of course, are appropriate behaviors in the pulpit.

A few years ago, a minister came to my church to speak, and he was very emotional. Some people would look at a preacher weeping and see it as a sign of his brokenness before God. And sometimes

that's true. Other times, it might not be brokenness but fatigue that's out of control. In this case,
that's what I felt it was. I pulled him aside and said,
"I'm your friend and I think you need to go rest.
You need to go back to your hotel, forget your
preaching schedule for the next two days. Sleep,
rest, eat, and be merry. And then let's talk about it."
It actually turned out to be a very good conversa-
tion. Sometimes the weeping and the emotions, or
the sense of heaviness, is out of tiredness and is
not a true burden of God.

My burden is light, so I know when I start
feeling too much of the human burden. I get more
prayer. I have personal intercessory prayer for me
before I preach every service. Four to six people
will minister to me for ten or fifteen minutes before I preach and that helps relieve any outside
stress I'm feeling. But if I'm too tired to think, too
tired to preach, too tired to handle it, I will back
out of the pulpit. I'll simply say, "Jack, Ken, Mark,

take Sunday. I'm over the line. I've got some emotions that are drained."

By learning to recognize the danger zones, you can take appropriate measures to avoid them. When you see one coming, give yourself time before sermons for personal prayer, intercessory prayer, or other measures that will take your mind off personal problems and move you into a loving spirit with focus on an appropriate teaching.

✦ **8. *The Law of Restrained Illustration***

Experiences of other people, appropriate jokes, great quotes on sermon subjects, and personal real-life incidents are wonderful tools to bring vitality to our sermons. We must connect biblical truths to current human condition; illustrations help us to apply these truths.

However, be extremely sensitive in using real-life incidents. If you're using a story involving another person in your family or congregation or on staff, always ask that person's permission before repeating the story from the pulpit. What may seem funny or impersonal or general knowledge to you could be considered extremely embarrassing or sensitive to the person involved. Don't take the chance of hurting them and possibly turning them away from the church as a result.

You are not primarily a storyteller but a truth teacher who uses illustrations to make the truth more understandable. Telling stories will get people's attention. If I start telling a story, I can see everybody look up—they are in. If it's a personal story, they are in even more. They want to know what happens. I have to be very careful not to use my wife or kids as illustrations. They don't like it, especially if I don't get their OK first. I don't reveal things that would put my son or daughter in a bad light. I continually wrestle with that because I know that what happened with Andrew would perfectly cinch a point I'm trying to make. But I have to let it go, and find another story that will make it happen.

Using stories and illustrations is an art, and it can be dangerous. Don't become a storyteller. Use stories only when it helps you be a better truth teller.

Author Richard Baxter warned in *The Reformed Pastor* of the dangers of relying too heavily on illustrations or humorous stories: "You cannot break men's hearts by jesting with them, or telling them a smooth tale, or patching up a gaudy oration. Men will not cast away their dearest pleasures upon a drowsy request of one that seemeth not to mean as he speaks, or to care much whether his request be granted."

Finally, always err on the side of caution in all illustrations; if you're concerned that a story or joke may offend someone, it probably will. Don't use it.

A PREACHER WHO PREACHES THE TRUTH UNCOMPROMISINGLY WILL BE ASKED, DOES YOUR PREACHING ALWAYS HAVE TO BE SO POINTED? DOES IT ALWAYS HAVE TO BE SO SHARP? AND OF COURSE THE ANSWER IS NO. HE CAN BLUNT HIS MESSAGE AND BECOME JUST AS DULL AS THE AVERAGE PREACHER.

— *Jesse Morrell, New England street preacher and author of "Cleansing the Temple"*

✦ **9.** ***The Law of Passion***

The preacher must have a strong passion for God, the message, and the people. To preach with passion is to preach with energy and emotion and conviction. Passion is evidence of a deep desire to spread the Gospel message, and true preaching is the ability to communicate the depth of those feelings. Author/minister Charles Spurgeon urged preachers to show their fervor in their sermons: "Preach not calmly and quietly as though you were asleep, but preach with fire and pathos and passion."

There is not enough fire and pathos in preaching today. Big hearts with big emotions make big preachers. The preacher binds the people to him by his heart, not his intellect. People may admire gifts and abilities but they will be moved by the passion of the preacher's heart.

We need fewer apathetic preachers. We need energy in the pulpit. The Gospel message is passionate, and we should preach it passionately. The British preacher G. Campbell Morgan put it this way: "Can a man preach these things without passion if they are truth to him? I cannot see how anyone really handles these things until he is handled by them. Painted fire never burns. And an imitated enthusiasm is the most empty thing that can possibly exist in a preacher."

✦ **10. The Law of Closing the Deal**

The length of the sermon will vary depending on the speaker, the audience, the event, the culture, or the country. The preacher must learn to recognize the intuitive feeling that "now" is the time to stop—and that's before droves of people start crowding the exits. The wise preacher will not complain about a shortened time period or stick to his planned message—all of it—no matter what else comes up. If time is short, abandon the low priority items in the message, no matter how much you agonized over them, and hammer out the major points. A sermon does not have to be eternal to be immortal.

The average sermon time today seems to be around 30 minutes. I remember the first time I preached at the Hillsong conference in Australia, the senior pastor Brian Houston told me I had 30 minutes and started a clock that was on the lectern. I was in the middle of a sentence when the clock's buzzer went off, so I turned it off, closed my Bible and said, "God be with you. I'm out of here."

The people laughed, but I did that every service. No matter where I was when the buzzer went off, I'd stop immediately. I have a hard time saying all I want to say within 30 minutes, but because I've taught in Bible college for so many years, I can stop in the middle of a sentence and close up a class. When the bell rings, the students don't sit there and say, "Go on, teacher. Go on." They are out the door. So I've learned to stop when my time is up and not get upset about it.

Each preacher must learn to recognize when to stop. One speaker requested help with his closing time this way: "I understand that it's my job to talk to you. I understand that it's your job to listen to me. If you quit before I do, I hope you'll let me know." It would be helpful to have a buzzer on every chair that people could punch when their attention span is gone; it would light up on your pulpit so you could see who you're losing. "Looks like I just lost that section over there. And this one is halfway down. It must be time to wrap up." That would help us a lot.

The ideal time to stop is when the message has been communicated and the anointing is strong. To go five or ten minutes beyond the "now" moment can change the atmosphere of the service and change the altar call or the response that you are looking for in the people. Long-winded speakers exhaust their listeners long before they exhaust their subjects.

Many years ago, a 40-minute to 55-minute sermon was the average. Go back a century or more, and some preachers would speak for several hours. The longest sermon on record was 48 hours and 18 minutes long. It was preached by Clinton Lacy of West Richland, Washington, in February of 1955 on the topic of the Beatitudes. In remarking on the length of that sermon, the preacher E. Eugene Williams observed: "Small wonder someone proposed the adoption of a new Beatitude: 'Blessed is the preacher whose train of thought has a caboose.'"

✦ 11. *The Law of Bonding*

The preacher must establish rapport with his listeners. Connecting to a congregation begins as connecting to a person; preaching is very much just that—connecting one person at a time. The connection happens when the listener can feel, see, and hear the personal warmth and caring of the preacher through his attitude and emotions, his thoughtfulness and openness.

By the same token, people can feel when the preacher is not genuine in his words or actions. Preachers should first be themselves and not an imitation of what they think a great preacher should look or sound like. And they must truly care for and about the people in their congregation and have a desire to personally know as many of them as possible. Love and compassion cannot be faked and the people will be cool to the message if the preacher's heart is cool toward them.

I find connecting is something I must do in my spirit before I ever get behind the lectern.

Before I start my message I will have a connecting thought and mood. I do not just get up and say, "Open your Bibles. Praise God. We're gonna preach the Word this morning." I try to start by coming around to the front of the pulpit, or off to the side, and making a general but personal comment: "Have you been busy? I don't know about you, but things have been hectic around here with graduations and summer break—kids coming and going." And the people think, "Ah, he's alive. He's real. He talked about summer in the pulpit." Then I say, "But you know what? God is so good, and this is going to be a great summer. It's fun to be in the house of God, isn't it? Come on, let's go to the Word this morning and let's talk about Jesus for a little bit."

Go to the pulpit with a feeling of confidence: *It's good to be alive and I love this church and I love this pulpit. This is a fantastic day just to be in the house of God.* That will come out in your preaching and people will join you in thinking it is a fun day to be alive.

But be yourself. I don't button my suit all the way up and open the big black Bible and use a preacher's voice and a preacher's stern look. That's not me. But you might connect with a preacher's suit, a preacher's voice, and a preacher's look, if that's you.

My father was a Baptist preacher and every time I ever saw him preach, he'd go to the pulpit, kneel down, put his face on the floor, and pray for his message. That's how he started every sermon. I guarantee you, it gets your attention. It did mine. Scared me all the years I was growing up, thinking, what disease he going to get down on the floor?

My dad is a very soft-hearted guy. He'd be on the floor sobbing about his message and the whole place would be broken up. The people would be moved deeply. When he stood up to preach there was no playing around. There was no illustration. There were no jokes. There was no "Hey, how's your day going?" It was straight to the heart, with the arrow, with the spear, with a hammer. Then he resurrected you and sent you home.

For my Dad that style worked. He could pray and preach like that and it worked for him. But if I did that, it wouldn't be genuine. My personality is more out front. I'm a friendly person and I want to communicate. I'll say things like, "Put on your slippers and robe, turn the coffee on, pull up to the fire. Let's talk." I like to make it personal. It's good for people to laugh. That way when you hit them in the teeth with truth, you don't split their lip.

Put your realness on the table. I'm a real man. Real life. Real Jesus. Let's talk about something that is real to all of us.

✦ 12. *The Law of Finishing Strong*

The conclusion of your message will determine its impact and the people's response. Be bold. Call for response. Be specific. The Word has been preached; believe that people are ready to respond. This is the part of the sermon most likely to be neglected. Just as athletes who finish strong can change the results of a race or game, so the preacher must be at his best in the closing minutes. [*See more on this subject in Part 2: Sermon Preparation.*]

✦ *13. The Law of Telling All*

The preacher may use personal experience to reflect on common struggles. The communication is: "I am human. I've been there. I understand." These personal illustrations should be used in a way to bring light to the word of God. Be wary of stories that tend to glorify or elevate yourself or trumpet your accomplishments. At the same time, be wary of glorifying your past failures or sins, making them seem appealing rather than flawed or erroneous.

While it is good to be open and personal with your listeners, there are parts of your life that should remain private. There are some sexual topics I won't talk about from the pulpit. I also won't talk about personal finance and investments. Our church has no clue what I do with my personal money. Not a clue. They would not have a clue whether I believed in the stock market or a certain kind of retirement plan, or if I own property. That is disclosure that I think will harm my message instead of help it.

Being honest and candid in the pulpit does not mean baring all or telling all. It does not mean being unwise, unguarded, or off-color.

✦ 14. *The Law of Bouncing Back*

A leader can encounter satanic attacks through unexpected circumstances, deviant harassment, or accumulated disapproval, criticism, censure, or questioning of motives by others. At these times, the leader may experience fear and loss of confidence, causing him to question his calling, his anointing, his placement, or his own heart.

These thoughts will only allow the enemy to take more ground. Instead, the preacher must know how to replenish his wellsprings with the living water of Jesus Christ through prayer, worship, reading the Word, and seeking trusted counsel. The preacher must continually replenish his strength in the Lord Jesus and have a resilient "comeback" spirit week after week.

✦ *15. The Law of Lifelong Learning*

Never think you have nothing left to learn about preaching. Success can become a great enemy of progress. When a preacher begins to believe every "Great sermon, pastor," he may feel he has perfected his preaching. This could also be called the "Law of Fresh Manna" as we may tend to live off yesterday's manna by repeating "golden oldie" topics.

No matter how good we get, or think we get, there's always room for improvement. Keep an eye on what's selling in Christian books and media to keep up with topics people are hungry for. Read new books and magazines on communications skills, linguistics, religion, philosophy, teaching, speaking, psychology, prayer. Grow, expand, read, pray, watch, listen. Never stop learning.

✦ **16. The Law of Constructive Criticism**

Every leader will at some point, or at many points, receive criticism from his listeners or from other preachers or church leaders. A preacher should not immediately take the criticism to heart, just as he must not accept all praise as a sign of his greatness. A leader must determine ahead of time to respond to a critical comment graciously, briefly, and without defensiveness. Later, when any initial emotional reaction has had time to dissipate, he or she should examine the comment and allow the Holy Spirit to reveal the truth of it and reveal any correction that should be made.

I've had many harsh things said to me over the years, but I can safely say, at this point in my journey, I believe there is no one who could criticize me and nothing they could say that would change my spirit. I don't let the criticism affect me.

Sometimes I'll say to people who have criticized me, when I know they can handle it: "That's small stuff. If you want something better to criticize me for, I'll give you some really juicy stuff." Or I'll say, "Oh, that's only one weakness of mine. I can give you five more that are a lot better than that." I no longer feel a need to defend myself nor to be defensive. It takes your critics by surprise when you say, "You may be right. Now let me tell you about my other flaws."

When I am criticized, I examine the content of what is said. I pray about it. I give it to God, and then I keep my spirit gracious. I will not allow any person to take my spirit.

✦ **17. The Law of Simplicity**

There is power and authority in being simple, precise, and to the point. The preacher must avoid complexity that breeds levels of confusion. Simplicity allows the listener to remember and apply what is being preached. It is better that people grasp one or two simple, direct thoughts than to be overwhelmed in a maze of points, illustrations, diagrams, or statistics. The Gospel message is simple and easy to understand. Your sermon should be the same.

Winston Churchill's famous declaration about the Royal Air Force in 1941 is a classic example of the impact of simple words: "Never in the field of human conflict was so much owed by so many to so few." They way he worded that, the way he brought that to the mind and spirit, shows his craftsmanship with words. To a simple subject and a simple style add simple words. If you're not certain what a word means and how it is used, don't use it. There is no point in speaking as if you swallowed a dictionary just to have a great vocabulary. The great preacher John Wesley understood the power of simplicity: "I design plain truth for plain people. I labor to avoid all words which are not easy to be understood. I preach in marketplace language."

If you're having trouble with a concept or word, try it out on your family. I've done that with my wife, and I admit that sometimes I don't like her response. I say, "Sharon, don't you understand what I just said?" She says, "No, Frank, I don't. You asked me to tell you and I just told you. I don't. Would you rather I just tell you that I did?" I say, "No, I want you to tell me that you don't. Let's try it this way. How about this way?" She says, "That makes more sense. Why didn't you say it that way to begin with?" I say, "Because I didn't have you."

✦ 18. *The Law of Spirit-Driven Speaking*

The preacher must be open to spontaneity in the message delivery. He must be open to the influence and power of the Holy Spirit to direct his thoughts, even when it is not tied to the message that has been carefully prepared. Be open to the inspiration of the moment. Some of the most important things a preacher says may not be premeditated or written out in the sermon material.

✦ 19. *The Law of Strategic Humor*

Humor is a wonderful tool to engage the attention of a congregation and set a positive, receptive atmosphere. But it should also be used with discretion. A preacher should never give the impression that the Gospel message is something light, superficial, or trivial. The preacher has a serious and sober challenge—the changing of people's lives for all eternity. If humor is used in

ONE REASON THE GATES OF
HELL ARE NOT FALLING BEFORE
THE CHURCH IS OUR LACK OF
BOLDNESS IN PREACHING. . . . WE
ARE NOT WIELDING THE SWORD
OF THE SPIRIT, BUT THE BATON
OF A CONDUCTOR.

— *Geoffrey Thomas,*
in The Preacher and Preaching

introducing people to that challenge, it must be used wisely.

The preacher Warren Wiersbe states, "If the preacher has a sense of humor, he had better dedicate it to the Lord and let the Spirit direct him in its use. For true humor can become a toy to play with, a tool to build with or a dangerous weapon to fight with."

+ 20. *The Law of Prayer-Filled Preaching*

The preacher who recognizes and applies the power of prayer in the preparation and the delivery of the sermon will be a more impacting preacher. Prayer in private makes preaching powerful in public. Prayer saturates the preacher with God's presence. It saturates the words, the scriptures, and the people. The process from topic idea to preaching the message must be surrounded and saturated by prayer. Prayer warrior/preacher

E. M. Bounds wrote, "Light praying will make light preaching. Prayer makes preaching strong and makes it stick."

✦ 21. *The Law of High Tech*

The technology of television, radio broadcast, video and film production, and now the Internet and portable media such as MP3 players and cellular devices have made it possible to spread the Gospel in every corner of our cities, nation, and world. Our own church is now using video simulcasts to transmit Sunday messages that will go live to three locations in two states and three cities, as well as Pod-casts that can be accessed internationally.

Preachers today must evaluate the use of drama, video, projected illustrations, simulcasts, broadcasts, web-casts, Pod-casts, and other technology in imparting the truth of the message. Again, these tools must not be used to turn the message into pure amusement, or for humor only, but to effectively spread the biblical word of God. The impact and effectiveness of media and technology must be measured by whether the message has penetrated the hearts of people through the power of the Holy Spirit, and not whether the people have been adequately entertained.

✦ **22. *The Law of Sowing the Seed***

The preacher must have patience and faith in the power of preaching the word of God. Preaching is like planting a seed; it takes time for a seed to germinate, grow, and produce fruit. God has promised that His word is never wasted and will not return void. It will penetrate the hardest heart. The preacher who does not see immediate results from his or her preaching must maintain faith and confidence that the seed has been planted and is growing under the surface. As additional seeds are spread in weekly sermons and fed by Bible studies, training, workshops, and prayer, the harvest will come. Do not become discouraged if you don't see instant results—the best crops grow from strong, deep roots.

Every one of you will excel in some area of the church. Why not excel in preaching? Why not excel in preaching the Word of God with such accuracy and fervency and intensity and penetration and feeding and knowledge of God that people will leave saying. "That was a life-changing hour in my life." You are not going to get there without enlarging your capacity, enlarging your desire, and setting a new bar of excellence to reach for.

Part 2

Sermon Preparation

There are as many methods of preaching as there are preachers. You may teach on a book of the Bible, done by chapter or by subject. You may teach on a chapter, in a verse-by-verse expository style. You may preach on a character of the Bible, revealing principles and insights for daily living. You could do place studies, such as Zion, the wilderness, or many others. You could do a thematic or subject study through the Scriptures to meet a particular need in the flock.

Which method do you typically use? Topical, textual, chapter study, theme study? How far ahead do you plan your preaching?

There are preaching calendars you can buy and plan the whole year of sermons around holidays, festivals, Pentacost, Easter, Mother's Day, summer series. I would not criticize that, but it doesn't take into consideration what is happening with your flock or with you. On Thanksgiving, your flock may need a patience message rather than a gratitude message. The weather may be hot, but your flock may not need a typical summer series.

I prefer to build sermon series to accomplish one thing I want to feed into the church. I'd rather feed a series of messages on prayer over four weeks or eight or sixteen weeks rather than a message on prayer one week, one on family the next, followed by one on the resurrection.

I prefer to take the flock, dip them in, take them out, shake them, dip them in, then out, shake them, shear them, dip again, take out, shake them, dip in a couple more times, get rid of the extra wool, take them out, look them in the eye, then hold them under until the subject and the truth have so absorbed into them it has become part of them and a part of the church. That's my method. Preaching is more enjoyable when you're grazing rather than flying through the fast-food lane.

Effective preaching is not in how you say it, it's how they get it. I try to make sure they get it.

The method that works for one preacher may not work for another when it comes to sermon preparation. Some preachers may prefer to outline; some to jot bullet points and scripture references; some to write out their message word for word. Some may prefer to start with research, then build the sermon, some to outline the sermon and then research the subject.

There are, however, certain elements common to all sermon planning: study, organization, illustration, communication. The process I've developed and used over the past 35 years of my preaching experience, from the beginning God-thought to the altar call, I will share below, not as the only or the perfect sermon

A GOOD SERMON IS AN
ENGINEERING OPERATION BY
WHICH A CHASM IS BRIDGED SO
THAT THE SPIRITUAL GOODS ON
ONE SIDE - THE UNSEARCHABLE
RICHES OF CHRIST - ARE
TRANSPORTED INTO PERSONAL
LIVES UPON THE OTHER.

—Harry Emerson Fosdick
Author, pastor, hymn writer (1878-1969)

planning procedure, but with the desire that some of my strategies may help you empower your own sermon planning.

Step One: Determining the subject

Determining the subject of the sermon is sometimes the most arduous step in the process. There are times that the idea comes like a bolt of lightning or a nudge from heaven. But more often, my experience is similar to that of Charles Spurgeon, who stated in *Lectures to My Students:* "I confess that I frequently sit hour after hour praying and waiting for a subject and that this is the main part of my study."

I have found there are some procedures I can employ to open my heart to receive sermon topics. These include:

- *Setting the atmosphere.* I have always enjoyed setting an atmosphere that results in the stirring of my spirit toward God and the Word. Prayer intermingled with worship music allows for the Spirit of God to move upon my mind and heart, preparing my spirit like a plowed field ready to receive the seed. This could bring ideas quickly or could be a time of waiting on the Lord. The God-thought must grow out of the soil of your soul and its roots must come from deep within your own experience, enhanced by your ability to hear the Holy Spirit and receive from God's written word.

❧ *The prophetic or rhema word.* I believe in the written word (*logos*) of God as the basis for all preaching and teaching. I also believe in the *rhema* word that arises out of the written word. The *rhema* word may be a scripture that the Spirit brings to our personal attention for use in time of need. A prerequisite to receiving a personally relevant word is to regularly store scripture in the mind. I find *rhema* words come to me out of meditating on certain portions of the Word: it may be one word or a phrase or a story or an event. This starts me on a journey of seeking God and asking for illumination. As Paul said in Galatians 1:11-12, "I want you to know, brothers, that the gospel I preached is not something that man made up. I did not receive it from any man, nor was I taught it; rather, I received it by revelation from Jesus Christ."

❧ *The topic journal.* I have found over the years there are many God-thoughts that come to me that I may not use immediately but will refer to at a later time for inspiration. A good discipline is to write these thoughts down in a "God-Thought" journal. You don't have to worry about what the idea means or try to develop each one as it comes, but simply put them into your treasure chest and wait for the right timing. I have God-thoughts that I have kept for literally years without developing them and yet when the seed is taken out of the box and planted, it brings forth fresh fruit immediately.

❧ *Messages from life's burdens.* Throughout Scripture we read about those who were burdened and from those burdens developed a word for their day. Many times my thought begins as a spiritual burden, something God puts into my spirit through experiences, observations, crises, problems, living life in a pressure cooker.

The burden could be something God is dealing with me about: a sin, a short-coming, a need in my own life or ministry. Or it could be a realization of spiritual conflict or a burden for another person or a need in our church congregation. Any or all of these may be developed into a message that is relevant to others going through similar experiences.

But as mentioned earlier in this book, be wary of using your personal difficulties as the topic of every sermon.

Step 2: Researching the topic

The research method I use is not a subjective process but a building block approach to developing the God-thought into a message—a biblical and practical way for the listeners to understand the word. The development of the topic can vary, depending on the nature of the idea—thematic, theological, historical, or biographical.

ֆ◈ *The topic developed by systematic research.*

If I have received a biblical word as part of my God-thought, then I will begin with a study on that particular word. For example, if the idea is found within the word "first," then I would go to my concordance and lay out a word study on "first," possibly finding other synonyms for first and looking them up as well. I don't try to interpret my thought before I finish my groundwork.

First I must finish with the word study and compile it into some order that will serve me in preparing the God-thought. The thought may be developed from a portion of scripture, a verse, chapter, or a whole book of the Bible. If this is the case, I will do an interpretation (exegesis) of the scriptures and build on biblical research. Exegesis

THE PREPARATION OF SERMONS
INVOLVES SWEAT AND LABOR AND
IS EXTREMELY DIFFICULT AT TIMES.

—*Martyn Lloyd-Jones*
Welsh evangelical preacher (1899-1981)

deals with the original languages of scripture (Hebrew and Greek) and builds on sound hermeneutical (interpretive) principles.

🐦 *Processing and structuring the study.*

I begin to put together a rough outline that organizes my thoughts about the God-word, which I am now seeing a little more clearly. As I have processed the thought through a word, passage, or some kind of word study, I have found some key elements, stories, or characters that could be used to develop a message.

My study will be put into an organized outline that allows me quick access to the biblical breadth of the subject. The God-thought may be developed as a word study, character study, place study, or an expositional study of scripture.

🐦 *Targeting and streamlining the topic.*

This is one of the hardest steps because I've typically had many ideas by now—not only the original God-thought, but also other quickened words that have surfaced along the way. If a preacher is not careful, he/she will end up chasing different words down different paths and either end up frustrated or losing the original thought in the ever-widening breadth of research.

It is important to narrow your approach to a specific passage, a specific historical event, or a specific character. At this point, I will have my first outline draft to aid me in streamlining and organizing my approach.

Step 3: Developing the topic into a study outline

I now move on to the message development with confidence and a sense of having a track to follow. I'm not double-minded about the direction I should take, and I'm not tempted to go into other interesting areas of study. I am focused and I have a study compass to guide me in my message outline. I can save time by working only on the areas within my study outline. If I take a side trip, I can easily get back on track. My research can now get serious.

❧ *Sample study outline*

I.   Define the word "First"
        Dictionaries
        Hebrew and Greek
        Other Sources
II. The First Things of Jesus
        Narrow topic to only the Gospels
        Research "first" things according to Jesus

The method of research will depend upon the kind of message I am developing. An expository message will demand different study techniques than a word-study-based message or a character-study-based message. If I choose the word "first" as the foundation to my message, then I would do a word study to find definitions and groupings of scriptures and thoughts on 'first."

As I go through my study outline, I research Hebrew and Greek dictionaries as well as any other sources to help define my key word. I then narrow the focus of the word "first" to the first things of Jesus. I choose seven key scriptures to develop into my main points:

> *Sample Sermon Outline: Scriptures of the Seven Firsts of Jesus*

- Matthew 6:33 - But seek first the kingdom of God and His righteousness, and all these things shall be added to you.

- Matthew 5:24 - Leave your gift there in front of the altar. First go and be reconciled to your brother; then come and offer your gift.

- Matthew 7:4-5 - How can you say to your brother, 'Let me take the speck out of your eye,' when all the time a plank is in your own eye? You hypocrite, first take the plank out of your own eye, and then you will see clearly to remove the speck from your brother's eye.

- Matthew 12:29 - Or again, how can anyone enter a strong man's house and carry off his possessions, unless he first ties up the strong man? Then he can rob his house.

- Matthew 22:36-38 - Teacher, which is the greatest commandment in the law? Jesus replied," 'Love the Lord your God with all your heart and with all your soul and with all your mind.' "This is the first and greatest commandment."

- Matthew 23:26 - Blind Pharisee! First clean the inside of the cup and dish, and then the outside will also be clean.

- Matthew 28:1 - After the Sabbath, at dawn on the first day of the week, Mary Magdalene and the other Mary went to look at the tomb.

Now that I have a set outline and my key words have been researched, I can move on to researching each section of my message. This is done keeping the main purpose of the message in the forefront of my mind at all times. I add to these points from other resources, commentaries, dictionaries, and articles pertaining to the subject.

It is wise to do what I call "layered research," covering each section of the message with a first layer of research and then going back and adding another layer as time allows. Without this strategy, you may spend all your time researching the first point and create an imbalanced message. Research the whole message at a general-knowledge level before going deeper on any one point.

Step 4: Developing the message outline

I organize my message in the areas of Introduction, Main Body, Illustrations, and Conclusion.

❧ *The Introduction.*

Generally my introduction and title of the message demand my full attention and take concentrated time to develop. I write the introduction out in one or two paragraphs, stating precisely what the listener can expect from this message and challenging some aspect of their heart to in-spire them to listen intently to the forthcoming message.

I start with two or three key passages (if my message is thematic). The congregation reads them aloud in one translation (usually projected on screen in a PowerPoint presentation) to bring unity of focus.

I then proceed to a short story, statistics, illus-trations, questions to ponder, or a real-life "Frank Damazio" experience. At this point, I should have the listener's attention, and they know what I am speaking on, why I am speaking on this sub-ject, and how they will benefit from this message. British minister John Henry Jowett said, "I have a conviction that no sermon is ready for preaching until we can express its theme in a short, pregnant sentence as clear as crystal."

Putting first things first is an issue at the heart of life. All of us feel torn by the things we want to do, by the demands placed on us, by the many responsibilities we have. Many people today could and do feel disoriented or confused. We may have no real sense of: What are the "first things"? What are the "first" and most important things in my life? Where do I find what is important? What should be my "first things" to live by?

Jesus gives us the wisdom for a life worth living. Jesus is able to summarize for us all of His teachings by using one word: first. Jesus summarizes the most important of all His parables, doctrines, and stories by giving us seven firsts to live by. He boiled it down, distilled thousands of teachings, writings, and theories into the one word: first. If we could grasp these core values, they would save us years of doubt, confu-

> sion, and misplaced energy. We would live
> a life with direction and satisfaction. If you
> want to be happy, do these things.

I then move on to the main body of my message. I generally preach from an outline of three to five main points. The first step is to form a general outline of the subject. At this stage, I am not concerned with how the outline is worded or if there is a rhythm to the thoughts, but I simply focus on the main points of the message. [See full sermon outline in Appendix A.]

After that is done, I begin the fine tuning on the specific preaching outline. Techniques that I use are alliteration, with each main point beginning with a specific letter, and rhythmic phrasing in which each phrase has the same "sound" to it.

The goal is to have points that are easily understood and easy to remember. Out comes my thesaurus as I search for words that clarify my points. This can take one or two hours in itself for refining the introduction and the preaching outline. Then I go back

THERE ARE SO MANY GOOD TOOLS FOR INNOVATIVE DELIVERY METHODS THAT IT SEEMS SILLY TO USE JUST ONE. JESUS USED DIALOGUE, METAPHOR, SIMILE, PARABLE, STORIES, OBJECT LESSONS, AND GENERALLY WHATEVER WAS HANDY.

— Pastor S. A. Shorrosh,
on www.mmmiblog.com

through the entire message again to add another layer with more supporting scriptures. Organization in a sermon must be a servant and not a master. The tension of form and function is always present. Among other details a preacher should consider in the message:

+ It is important to be precise, to the point and exacting. Be specific in Bible references, quotations, dates, articles, and facts of any kind; give the sources of quotes or statistics in your message. If your facts aren't correct, the listeners may question the substance.

+ Bring your message into the present. A preacher who lingers in the past too long will run the risk of losing the people's interest and missing the mark of preaching—changed lives. The purpose of preaching is to discover the timeless truths and principles within the word of God, express them in 21st century language, and apply them to the needs of present people.

+ Speak to the listener as if you were alone with them. Lean over the pulpit and say something like, "Here we are again. Let's talk about what's going on in your soul and mine."

+ The reading of the word of God in different translations will feed the spirit and the mind. A specific translation may help to clarify or expand upon a particular passage to better get your point across.

❧ *Sample Sermon Points - The Firsts of Jesus*

- First seek the kingdom of God: Renewing Kingdom lifestyle (Matt. 6:33)

- First be reconciled with your brother: Repairing faulty relationships (Matt. 5:24-25)

- First remove the log from your own eye: Remove judgmental attitudes (Matt. 7:4-5)

- First bind the strong man: Recovering stolen goods (Matt. 12:29)

- First the greatest commandment: Reviving passion for God (Matt. 22:36-38)

- First cleanse the inside of the cup: Renouncing destructive sins (Matt. 23:26)

- First day of the week began to dawn: Respecting the Lord's Day (Matt. 28:1; Heb 10:25)

Next I focus on illustrations. The stories and illustrations used to make a message impacting and alive must be carefully planned by the preacher. The preacher should have a treasure chest filled with great illustrations and an organized method to access this material. There are many books as well as Internet websites that are good sources for topical stories and illustrations.

If done wisely, one of the best ways to illustrate is to use personal, real-life stories. It is always best to get the approval of anyone mentioned in the story if possible. Think through the emotion you are interjecting in the story as well as how you will exit the story without losing the message momentum.

It is easy to get carried away with stories or illustrations that may end up detracting from the central message. Remember that God's Word is the point of the message and that it will change lives. Stories or illustrations must support the Word, not distract from it.

〜 *The conclusion.*

The conclusion of the message should be carefully thought through, prayed through, and talked through. I will preach the whole message aloud to myself on "fast forward," seeking to gauge the impact of the message and how best to bring it to a conclusion. Bringing it to a close, ending, and shutting up are what I must accomplish. I must bring the listener to a decision to apply the message.

I personally like to end my message with a definite goal in mind, a response to the Word that is direct, brief, bold, and Holy Spirit-driven. Altar calls are awkward for some preachers, who fear no one will respond. But we should leave that up to God.

We may ask for response for salvation, prodigals, healing, help, encouragement, and/or prayer of agreement. Whatever the purpose, do it with faith and directness. Know what you want to accomplish. Prepare your words carefully in your message notes and then launch out. The Holy Spirit will confirm God's word. God has prepared people for your message.

Questions to Ask in Evaluating Your Preaching

Once you have completed your sermon preparation, use the following questions to evaluate your message and presentation.

❧ *Evaluating the Structure*

- ✦ Was it the mind of God—something you knew God wanted communicated?

- ✦ Was it well prepared?

- ✦ Was it biblical in aim and in content?

- Does your sermon have movement to it? A forward motion? A flow?

- Does your sermon have unity to it?

- Does your sermon have definite points and parts? Do you spend sufficient time on each part?

- Does your sermon have a clear, central point? Is it easy to remember? Is it stated clearly?

Evaluating the Message

- Is it biblical?

- Is it true?

- Is it relevant to this audience (helpful, understandable)?

- Do the illustrations relate to the key points?

- Is it compassionate?

- Is it logical? Is there an easily followed structure?

+ Is it interesting?

+ Is there a call to some kind of action?

❧ *Evaluating the Messenger (ask someone to help you with this part)*

+ Does he/she have authority?

+ Is the preacher a real person (vulnerable, human)?

+ Does the preacher love the congregation or just love to preach?

+ Is the preacher a learner with the congregation or a remote teacher (pompous, pious)?

+ What do the preacher's body language and face communicate (love, anger, joy, nervousness)?

+ Does the preacher have energy and excitement?

+ Is the preacher an original or a copy?

IT IS A POOR SERMON THAT GIVES
NO OFFENSE; THAT NEITHER MAKES
THE HEARER DISPLEASED WITH
HIMSELF NOR WITH THE PREACHER.

— *George Whitfield*

Part 3

The Preacher and the Word of God

The great British preacher G. Campbell Morgan made a commitment to read and study only the Bible and no other book each day until one o'clock in the afternoon. Joseph Parker, preacher and author of the 25-volume *Preaching Through the Bible*, went to his study at 7:30 every morning and read the Scriptures for four hours. He did this six days a week for more than 30 years. He would read the Bible for four hours, then have a cup of tea. Then he would take an hour walk and meditate on what he had read. Then he would start research. But first he read the Bible.

Most of us don't read the Bible enough. We read everything else first. There are a hundred different magazines coming to my house and my office. If I were to read all the Christian magazines I get, I would never have time to pick up the Bible again in my life. I tell my secretary, "Please don't show me any more magazines. I'll see something that catches my interest and read what other people think about it. I need to read what God thinks."

We are in the God business. The preacher is called to preach the Word of God. There are many temptations to preach on contemporary or secular topics and end up neglecting the powerful, living word of God. Preaching the Word can be unpopular in this entertainment-oriented, short-attention-span generation, but preaching the Word is essential if we are to fulfill our calling.

The greatest power ever known is the Word of God. It has called worlds into being, toppled empires, healed and comforted the sick, shaken the proud, and resurrected the dead.

For the word of God is living and powerful. Sharper than any two-edged sword, it penetrates even to dividing soul and spirit, joints and marrow; it judges the thoughts and attitudes of the heart (Heb. 4:12).

This scripture makes it clear: God's word is alive, powerful, and relevant today. It penetrates the dividing line of our life/soul and our eternal spirit. It penetrates even the deepest parts of our nature (joints and marrow), reveals our doubts and defenses, examines and judges the thoughts and intentions of our hearts.

When you preach the Word of God, that Word is going deep into the crevices of people's souls, discerning, cutting, judging, expanding, energizing , exposing every little detail. It is touching things that you don't even know exist in their souls.

I read Scripture with my church every Sunday because it gives the Holy Spirit at least two or three things to work with. If nothing else is as good as what I read from the Bible, at least He can take that and work with it.

PASTOR, WHEN YOUR PEOPLE
GATHER, THEY NEED TO HEAR FROM
GOD. THEY HAVE BEEN HEARING
ALL SORTS OF MESSAGES ALL WEEK
LONG; THEY NOW NEED TO HEAR
A MESSAGE FROM HIS WORD.

— *Ron Owens,*
in Return to Worship:
A God-Centered Approach

I've listened to preachers who never opened their Bible during the service. I've listened to preachers who never quote a Scripture. I've listened to preachers who, in my mind, are preaching themselves—their experiences, their opinions, their ideas, and throwing in a few God thoughts along the way. Some of it is very funny. Some of it is very emotional. But where is the Word? You can almost see the Holy Spirit saying, "Just one. I just want one Scripture. Sermon is over, not even one. I didn't even get to work on one person with one Scripture all service."

The Living Word

No one is unaffected by God's word—we must listen, as Martin Luther, the Reformation and Protestant leader, expressed with great passion: "The Bible is alive, it speaks to me; it has feet, it runs after me; it has hands, it lays hold on me."

The Bible must be alive to preachers, must speak to us. The Word of God has an answer for everything. In our culture, I believe there is a lurking doubt about the validity of the Bible. You might not have people say it to you, but it is in a lot of their minds: "The Bible doesn't really answer everything." Or, "The Bible is not always accurate." And, "The Bible doesn't address contemporary times and issues."

The Bible is truth, all truth, and it can speak to any area of life. The Word of God is Holy and instructive. As Paul wrote in 2 Timothy 3:16-17: "All Scripture is God-breathed and is useful for teaching, rebuking, correcting and training in righteousness, so that the man of God may be thoroughly equipped for every good work."

The Bible is the Word of God in such a way that, when the Bible speaks, God speaks. I say that to my church. When the Bible speaks, God speaks. The ultimate author of Scripture is God himself. The Bible is God's word, written. Every word of it. The more you say that to the church, the more the church will respond to your preaching.

Four Keys to Effective Biblical Preaching

Biblical preaching should penetrate the heart and soul of the listeners and produce changes in their lives. But as the apostle Paul stated in 1 Corinthians 2:1-5, the power of preaching is not in the preacher's wisdom or eloquence, but in the Holy Spirit and the word of God:

> When I came to you, brothers, I did not come with eloquence or superior wisdom as I proclaimed to you the testimony about God. For I resolved to know nothing while I was with you except Jesus Christ and him crucified. I came to you in weakness and fear, and with much trembling. My message and my preaching were not with wise and persuasive words, but with a demonstration of the Spirit's power, so that your faith might not rest on men's wisdom, but on God's power.

The central message here is that we as preachers do not make the word of God powerful. The word of God is powerful without the help of our human knowledge or smooth speaking style. This does not mean, though, that we should not prepare our sermons or messages ahead of time and instead depend on the Holy Spirit to feed us words when we stand before the church. We need to make our best effort to present the Gospel message with clarity and with passion, and this requires considerable research, study, and prayer before we take the stage. Good preaching is cooked in a crockpot, not a microwave. Don't feed your sheep fast food with no nutrition—they'll wonder why they're hungry again two hours later.

Filling, successful, effective preaching must have four essential ingredients:

❧ Edification

Biblical preaching should be encouraging. It should strengthen, or edify, the listeners through biblical principles. Edifying preaching builds up and improves. It increases and strengthens faith and spiritual life: Say to those with fearful hearts, *"Be strong, do not fear; your God will come (Isa. 35:34)."*

Edifying preaching praises, consoles, encourages, and comforts the flock with well-chosen words and a Christ-like spirit.

❧ *Revelation*

Revelation refers to unveiling, making visible that which is hidden to the eye. Our preaching must reveal and make manifest the word of God through messages that bring light through simplicity and clarity.

❧ *Inspiration*

Sermons should be reflections of our convictions, not our opinions. The preachers' responsibility is to proclaim what they perceive to be the Word of God. Anyone bold enough to enter a pulpit to speak for God should hold strong convictions that have been reached through inward struggle, biblical research, prayer, and openness to the Holy Spirit. The Greek word for inspiration, theopneustos, means "the breath of God." The Word of God is a source of life, a divine vitality, in contrast to human writings, which may give a temporary lift but do not give life.

Inspired preaching may also be prophetic. Prophecy is a word coming from divine inspiration to declare the mind of God in any situation. Prophetic preaching at times comes to the people as a challenge, a confrontation, a diagnosis of a spiritual problem with the proper prescription. Prophecy is also given to strengthen, encourage, and comfort (1 Cor. 14:3).

❧ Instruction

Instructive preaching is systematic, organized, carefully thought-through material that is developed to meet a specific need. Doctrine is specifically instructions or taught principles or a system of beliefs accepted as authoritative. It comes from the root word that means one who "stands over," such as a superintendent or doctor. Jesus was considered an authoritative teacher:

When Jesus had finished saying these things, the crowds were amazed at his teaching, because he taught as one who had authority, and not as their teachers of the law. (Matt. 7:28-29)

The chief priests and the teachers of the law heard this and began looking for a way to kill him, for they feared him, because the whole crowd was amazed at his teaching. (Mark 11:18)

Preachers preach with authority when they preach the Word of God. John Wesley once said, "I want to know one thing – the way to heaven. . . . God himself has condescended to teach the way. He hath written it down in a book. O give me that Book! At any price, give me the book of God!"

That quote should be on every pastor's desk. Give me the book. Give me the book that has in it the only eternal truth of any book in all of Barnes and Noble, in all the libraries of the world. There is only one book that throbs with life—the Bible. The only book that will do for you and I what we know needs to be done is the Bible. Preach the Word.

Part 4

The Preacher as Feeder of the Flock

A preacher has to develop tools and skills for preaching in a multitude of situations, but he also has to have a heart for the people he leads. When God took David from the sheep pens to become a shepherd of his people, David shepherded them "with integrity of heart; with skillful hands" (Psalm 78:72).

Those two characteristics—integrity of heart and skillfulness—are key to preaching effectiveness. Sometimes preachers will have more of one of these characteristics than the other. One may be a heart preacher who has great integrity and love for the people but doesn't have the skill to present the Word. Another may be very skilled, academically prepared, have years of training and experience in hermeneutics, homiletics, exegesis, exposition, laws, science, and arts, but have no heart for feeding the people of God. Leaders must strive to find a balance between their word ministry of teaching, preaching, training, and prophecy and their caring ministry of counseling, relationship-building, visiting, and loving concern.

Some preachers love their preaching more than they love the people and it affects the feeding of their flock. <u>Preachers should be focused on what they want their sheep to eat rather than how well they're going to preach</u>. Preachers should be more interested in the food they're putting into people rather than how it is being served.

Are you a good feeder? Does your congregation feel fed? When your people leave the church, are they full or still hungry? Do they say, "That was a full meal deal—I got the appetizer, I got the main course, I got the dessert. I've been fed so well, I'm stuffed. Thank you, pastor."

Nutritious Food

The food provided in the Word of God never changes: it is pure, powerful, and always in line with the needs of the people. This is not always the case with the feeder of the flock. Many pastors and teachers are under a lot of pressure and frustration in the area of feeding. Some shepherds are discouraged because of their lack of training, others by their lack of time.

What kind of food are you cooking? What kind of feeder are you? There is a difference between a preacher and feeder. You can be a good preacher but not feed well. You can feed well but not be a great preacher. It is possible to be both.

I love the Bible. I love Jesus. I love the Word. Most of the time, I love people. Most of the time, I enjoy feeding people. It's not always easy to do, but Jesus made it clear: "If you love me, feed my sheep." Jesus was first a shepherd, then a preacher. First a savior and second a preacher. Do you love Him? Then feed His sheep.

The Bible is firm on this point:

> *Be shepherds of God's flock that is under your care, serving as overseers—not because you must, but because you are willing, as God wants you to be . . . eager to serve, not lording it over those entrusted to you, but being examples to the flock. And when the Chief Shepherd appears, you will receive the crown of glory that will never fade away (1 Pet. 5:2-4).*

> *Keep watch over yourselves and all the flock of which the Holy Spirit has made you overseers. Be a shepherd of the church of God, which he bought with his own blood (Acts 20:28).*

> *Then I will give you shepherds after my own heart, who will lead you with knowledge and understanding (Jer. 3:15).*

The Serving Demands on a Preacher

Not long ago, an international pastor told me, "The preachers in America are stagnant. They don't pray and they don't study. The reason they don't grow is that they're serving the wrong table."

Some of us preachers are like waiters at rush hour, serving so many tables that we're spilling coffee, mixing up orders, breaking dishes, and we're worn out by the end of the week. We sit down on Saturday and say, "Help me God—you've got to help me preach tomorrow. They're *your* people."

Sometimes when I go to my study to start preparing my sermon, I'm so frazzled with confrontation and irritation and busy work that I sit down and fall asleep. My wife will walk in and say, "Waiting on the Lord, dear?" I'm so drained that preaching is beyond my grasp. My heart's not right; my schedule's not right—I'm spending all my energy serving the wrong tables.

Then the twelve summoned the multitude of the disciples and said, "It is not desirable that we should leave the word of God and serve tables" (Acts 6:2).

Preachers are pressured to serve a lot of different tables: conflict resolution, building projects, personnel, training, budgeting, administration, church growth, counseling, and multiple church and outreach programs. Some preachers get wrapped up in the small stuff; they get more discouraged over a mistake in the bulletin than sin in the church. They'll be reading the bulletin right before giving the message, and be thinking, "It's so ugly. And there's another misspelled word. And that's the wrong announcement the third Sunday in a row. I'm going to get my hands on the bulletin person. . ." Then it's time for him to preach, and he grits his teeth and says to himself, "Yes, I love my sheep. I love to feed my sheep."

Another wrong table to serve is that of meeting every person's expectations of you. Whether you serve 50 people or 100 people or 4,000 people, there are going to be many, many times that you will not meet their expectations—and you'll hear about it. People want to have dinner with you. They come in and say, "I want to meet with you for prayer one morning every week." They say, "What do you do with all your time?" They think you only work a couple hours on Sunday morning and nap the rest of the week. You have an urge to lay hands on them to heal their minds. Or they say, "Our last pastor used to always have time to have dinner with us." Or "Our pastor always came to our kids' games."

AT SOME POINT YOU HAVE TO BUY INTO THE FACT THAT YOU SHOULD TAKE OFF THE APRON AND PUT ON THE MANTLE.

I'm the type of person who would like to do those things. I wish I could. But if I did, I wouldn't have any energy left to serve the tables I should be serving. I have to tell people, in a nice way, that I'm not going to meet all their expectations. I have trained leaders who can counsel with them and pray with them and lay hands on them.

Every decision to be made in your church can't come to you. It will not serve your people to be at their disposal. At some point you have to buy into the fact that you should take off the apron and put on the mantle. Other people are called to put on the apron. They are called to serve that table.

The Two Tables All Preachers Should Serve

Preachers must pray and they must spread the Gospel. Those two tables preachers must serve above all others. As Paul says in Acts 6:4, We will give our attention to prayer and the ministry of the word.

One of many great prayer warriors in the ministry was John Knox, founder of the Presbyterian Church in Scotland. As he lay weakened and bed-ridden at the end of his life, Pastor Knox had his wife read to him Jesus' prayer in John 17. Then Knox began to pray fervently for his fellow man. He pleaded for those who had thus far rejected the gospel. He prayed on behalf of the recently converted for a firm foundation and steady growth in spirit. And he requested protection for those serving in the Lord's kingdom work, especially those facing persecution for their faith. As Knox prayed in intercession for all these, his spirit went home to be with the Lord. Queen Mary had said of John Knox, "I fear his prayers more than I do the armies of my enemies." Knox ministered through those powerful prayers until his final breath.

Prayer is a Necessity

Prayer is not an option for preachers; it is a necessity. As Rev. "Praying" Edward Payson said almost two centuries ago: "Prayer is the first thing, the second thing, the third thing necessary to a minister. Pray, then, my dear brother; pray, pray, pray."

Many other preachers over the decades have extolled the power of prayer in their ministries:

"Light prayer will make for light preaching."

— Alexander Whyte, 20th-century Scottish minister and professor

"Give yourselves to prayer, and get your texts, your thoughts, your words from God."

— Robert Murray McCheyne, 19th-century Scottish evangelical preacher

"The superficial results of many a ministry, the deadness of others, are to be found in the lack of praying. No ministry can succeed without much praying, and this praying must be fundamental, ever-abiding, ever-increasing."

— E.M. Bounds, 19th-century Methodist minister and writer

"If you lose your spirit of prayer, you will do nothing or next to nothing although you had the intellectual endowment of an

angel. The blessed Lord deliver and pre-
serve his dead church from the guidance
and influence of men who know not what
it is to pray."

— Charles Finney, 19th-century revival
   preacher; sometimes spent a full day
   in prayer prior to preaching

"The value of consistent prayer is not that
He will hear us, but that we will hear Him."

— William McGill, "Prayer Unceasing,"
   Living Church

"Knee work! Knee work!"

— Charles Spurgeon, preacher and author,
   when asked the secret of spiritual
   power

"Start, continue and end with prayer. For
in his study the prophet can build his altar and on it lay the wood. There he can
lovingly place his sacrificed sermon, but
still he knows the fire must come down

from God. Come it will, if he prays before he works and if he works in the spirit of prayer."

— Andrew Blackwood, professor of homiletics, Princeton Theological Seminary

"God does nothing but in answer to prayer."

— John Wesley, Anglican clergyman and co-founder of Methodism.

"If I fail to spend two hours in prayer each morning, the devil gets the victory through the day."

— Martin Luther, Reformer and Protestant leader, 16th century

"Prayer and patience and faith are never disappointed. I have long since learned that if ever I was to be a minister, faith and prayer must make me one."

— Richard Newton, 19th-century preacher and writer

While Jesus is our definitive role model in terms of prayer, another who understood and took to heart Jesus' exhortation to pray without ceasing was John Vassar, an early American missionary for a Christian literature company.

Vassar, as reported by an acquaintance, "absolutely prayed day and night—prayed about everything, prayed for almost everything, prayed with almost everybody he met. He prayed when he went out and when he came in. He prayed before every religious service, and then prayed all the way through it. I have occupied the same room with him night after night, and rarely went to sleep without hearing him in prayer, or awoke without finding him in prayer." Vassar saved thousands of men, women, and children in one-on-one encounters (some would say confrontations of souls) and was never an ordained minister.

How much more could we do if we devoted as much time and energy to intercessory prayer?

IF SINNERS BE DAMNED, AT LEAST
LET THEM LEAP TO HELL OVER
OUR BODIES. IF THEY WILL PERISH,
LET THEM PERISH WITH OUR ARMS
ABOUT THEIR KNEES. LET NO
ONE GO THERE UNWARNED AND
UNPRAYED FOR.

— *Charles Spurgeon,*
19th-century Anglican preacher and writer

The Priority of the Word

In addition to prayer, the second table the preacher must serve is teaching the Gospel, the ministry of the Word of God. English preacher and writer Charles Spurgeon said it is the preacher's challenge "to eat into the very soul of the Bible until at last you come to talk scriptural language and your spirit is flavored with the words of the Lord, so that your blood is biblical blood and the very essence of the Bible flows from you."

Knowing and studying the Bible until you can speak it from your heart and until the "very essence" of the Bible flows through you should be the goal of every preacher. Biblical teachings on the power of the Word underscore this crucial table a preacher must serve:

❧ *He humbled you, causing you to hunger and then feeding you with manna, which neither you nor your fathers had known, to teach you that man does not live on bread alone but on every word that comes from the mouth of the Lord (Deut. 8:3).*

≥ *As for God, His way is perfect; the word of the Lord is flawless; He is a shield for all who take refuge in Him (Ps. 18:30).*

≥ *I have hidden your word in my heart, that I might not sin against you (Ps. 119:11).*

≥ *Holding fast the word of life, so that I may rejoice in the day of Christ that I have not run in vain or labored in vain (Phil. 2:16).*

Keeping the Sheep's Attention

If the sheep don't absorb what you're feeding them, it could signify a problem with the sheep instead of the shepherd. Good learners are prepared listeners. Hungry listeners are prepared to receive by giving their attention 100 percent.

Unfortunately, most preachers do not have congregations full of great listeners. Most have at least a few of the following:

- The Uninterested: This type is bored, apathetic, emotionless. His jaded expression remains the same through worship, prayer, humor, pathos, altar call, dismissal.

- The Detailer: He's overly concerned with minute details and misses the main point.

- The Criticizer: She criticizes the speaker's delivery, voice, topic, weight, hair style, or any other handy target.

- The Outliner: His only flexibility is with the color of pen he uses for taking notes. Everything must fit into his outline format.

- The Overstimulated: Each point sends this receiver out on a private wave frequency to assorted off-track pathways or a flurry of text-messaging.

- The Distracter: Creates disturbances by moving around, cracking gum, stretching, digging through handbag, rustling papers, whispering, checking watch. Misses the message of the speaker and causes others to miss it also.

- ❧ The Lazy-Minded: Cannot tolerate using the gray matter. Avoids listening to difficult material.

- ❧ The Biased: Maintains firm personal judgments against specific words, people, thoughts, doctrines, interpretations, and anything else that gets in his path.

Teaching Listening Skills

Key elements in good listeners are spiritual hunger, a desire to understand the Word, and a prepared spirit through prayer. A perfect example of this type of listener is found in chapter 8 of Nehemiah. After completing the rebuilding of the wall of Jerusalem, all the men and women of the area gathered in the square and asked the priest Ezra to read to them from God's Law. As Ezra stood on the platform and opened the book, all the people stood up in anticipation of the coming words. Ezra then praised God, and all the people responded by lifting their hands and shouting "Amen! Amen!"

Ezra read from "daybreak till noon," while "all the people listened attentively." Afterward, the people celebrated "because they now understood the words that had been made known to them."

That kind of anticipation and attention from our listeners today would probably make most preachers speechless from the shock. However, it is possible to instruct people to become more attentive listeners and therefore more effective learners.

Among practical measures leaders may take to create a better listening atmosphere:

❧ Encourage people to move closer to the front if seats are available. It is easier to establish rapport with listeners you can see and make eye contact with. Those closer to the front are also more likely to participate and become emotionally involved in praise and worship, as well as prayer, and thus open to the presence of the Holy Spirit and a desire to hear the word of God.

❧ Ask for a response from your listeners. If you're preaching on humility, ask "How many of you think you might still have some ego problems you need to work on?" or "How many of you know someone who might have some ego problems they need to work on?"

❧ Ask your listeners to repeat a key point. I'll say to them, "Tell the person on your right: 'You need to be more patient.'" Or "Say to your neighbor, 'You need to pray more.'"

❧ Suggest that your listeners highlight key information in writing. When your listener is asked to take physical action, it will keep her or him on track. I'll say, "write down these four points." Or "underline these three words in your Bible." Or I'll ask them to "put your hand on your heart" or "reach out and grab your breath" in order to make a point—and keep them involved.

- At the beginning of each sermon, and sometimes during the sermon, I'll have everyone read aloud the key scriptures. Since there are many different Bible translations used among the 4,000-plus members of our church, we now have the verses projected on screen so that everyone is reading the same wording.

- Use charts or slides for sermon points. If you have the technology, use presentation software to project your Bible references and key information—or overhead projectors or dry-erase boards. Having the information you're giving orally from the pulpit repeated in visual form will help your listeners stay focused. Just be wary of making the props too much of a sideshow that would detract from your preaching rather than enhance it.

Helping your congregation listen will improve the experience and the effectiveness for both you and them. By making it a two-way communication, listeners feel more involved and as a result will be more attentive and more likely to receive the message through the Spirit.

As Jesus told his disciples in Matthew 13:16-17, "Blessed are your eyes because they see, and your ears because they hear. For I tell you the truth, many prophets and righteous men longed to see what you see but did not see it, and to hear what you hear but did not hear it." ✣

HOW SHALL THEY BELIEVE IN HIM
OF WHOM THEY HAVE NOT HEARD?
AND HOW SHALL THEY HEAR
WITHOUT A PREACHER?

Romans 10:14

Appendix A: Sample Sermon Outline

Following is a complete sermon outline from a series I preached at City Bible Church in Portland, Oregon, on "Kingdom Priorities: The Seven 'Firsts' of Jesus." This series was later developed into a book, *The Power of Spiritual Alignment: Living According to the Seven Firsts of Jesus.*

[To order a CD set that includes the entire "Seven Firsts of Jesus" sermon series on audio CDs, with printable sermon notes and digital files of PowerPoint slides included, visit www.CityChristianPublishing.com or check the product information at the back of this book.]

First Seek the Kingdom:
Renewing Kingdom Lifestyle

- ❧ We all struggle
- ❧ We all feel the tension
- ❧ We all know we want to change
- ❧ We all love God and would like to love God more
- ❧ Things have changed over time.

> Set your heart first on His kingdom and His goodness and all these things will come to you as a matter of course. But you must make His kingdom and uprightness before Him your greatest care and all will be yours over and above. (Matthew 6:33)

> No one can serve two masters; for either he will hate the one and love the other, or else he will be loyal to the one and despise the other. You cannot serve God and mammon. (Matthew 6:24)

Introduction

A woman once said to E. Stanley Jones, "Dr. Jones, you are obsessed with the kingdom of God." His reply: "I wish that were true because that would be a magnificent obsession." One philosopher said of life appraisal, "An unexamined life is not worth living." We are seeking to appraise our lives by studying the words of Jesus. The seven "firsts" stated by Jesus become a measuring rod for us to evaluate our life quality and life fulfillment. My intention is to ignite your passion for God and to encourage you to return to your first love, Jesus.

❧ "Much of our activity these days is nothing more than a cheap anesthetic to deaden the pain of an empty life."

❧ Knowing is Not Enough: "Several years ago Dr. Gordon A. Alles, noted chemist who pioneered the development of insulin for the treatment of diabetes, died of that very disease. Friends of Dr. Alles said he either did not know he had the disease or he kept the knowledge to himself. He collapsed in a diabetic coma in his home and died soon after in a local hospital in Pasadena, California. Dr. Alles did considerable research on insulin, helping to purify it sufficiently for human use. Certainly, of all people, he knew how to treat the disease. And if he had knowledge of his own condition, his death was even more tragic. For Dr. Alles, knowing how to treat the disease was not enough."

❧ Thomas Kelly on Focus: "The outer distractions of our interests reflect an inner lack of integration in our own selves. We are trying to be several selves at once without all our selves being organized by a single, mastering Life within us."

I. First Seek the Kingdom of God

A.   Translations of Matthew 6:33

   1.   NKJ: Seek first the kingdom of God and His righteousness, and all these things shall be added to you.

   2.   Amplified: But seek (aim at and strive after) first of all His kingdom and His righteousness (His way of doing and

being right), and then all these things taken together will be given you besides.

3. Phillips: Set your heart first on His kingdom and His goodness and all these things will come to you as a matter of course.

4. Guest: But be seeking first the kingdom and His goodness and all these things, all of them, shall be added to you.

5. Weymouth: But make His kingdom and righteousness your chief aim and then these things shall all be given you in addition.

6. Young's Literal: But seek ye first the reign of God and His righteousness and all these shall be added to you.

7. Godspeed: But you must make His kingdom and uprightness before Him, your greatest care and all will be yours over and above.

8. Barclay: Make the Kingdom of God and life in loyalty to Him, the object of all your endeavor, and you will get all these other things as well.

B. The Importance of Renewing a Kingdom Lifestyle

George Barna: "When individuals are single-minded in their devotion to God, then commitment to His ways and His principles becomes much deeper, much more intense. Once they have made an enduring and serious commitment then the peripherals don't matter as much."

1. It shapes our moral and ethical convictions.

2. It directly affects our response to pain and hardship.

3. It gives us strength when we are tempted.

4. It keeps us faithful and courageous when we face impossible odds.

5. It determines our lifestyle and dictates our philosophy.

6. It gives meaning and significance to relationships.

7. It stimulates hope to go on regardless.

8. It aligns our lives with biblical priorities.

II. Far-reaching Effects of What We Seek First

Read Matthew 6:25-34 [with church on screen]

A. The Word Seek

- The disciples too will seek but they will seek something that is far beyond the thought of the heathen world.

- Seek: implies a being absorbed in the search for, a persevering and strenuous effort to obtain, be constantly seeking. To seek means on our part, to seek, to obtain and enjoy.

B. The Wrong Choice: Seeking the wrong things results in worry (Matt. 6:25)

- Worry comes from an old German word meaning to strangle or choke. Worry is a mental and emotional strangulation.

- Worry is a thin stream of fear that trickles through the mind which, if encouraged, will cut a channel so wide that all other thoughts will be drained out.

1. Worry is sin. It distrusts the promises and providence of God.

2. Worry is irreverent. It fails to recognize God as the master controller of all things.

3. Worry is irrelevant. It does not change things, nor does it help us cope with problems.

4. Worry is irresponsible. It burns up our spiritual energy.

5. Worry is the opposite of contentment. (Phil. 4:11-12; 1 Tim. 6:6-8)

6. Worry is unreasonable because of our faith.

7. Worry is setting our hearts on materialism.

    C.   The Right Choice: Seeking the right things results in peace (Matt. 6:33)

        1.   Lenski: He who seeks the kingdom first will seek other things from the father in the right way, by humble and submissive prayer, without worry, without false estimate of these things that are of necessity for living but must be kept in the right place.

        2.   Scriptures: Philippians 4:6-7; 1 Peter 5:7; Lamentation 3:22-23; Isaiah 26:3-4

        3.   True believers seek first God's kingdom, not simply to refrain from the pursuit of temporal things but to replace such pursuits with goals of greater significance.

III. Marks or Evidences of Seeking First

❧ Watchman Nee: "A spiritual man is not a man born again, but a man born again and walking in alignment."

- First (Gr): first in time and number, first in rank and value, the most important.

- First (Dictionary): foremost in place, preceding all others in number, the first thing, that which is before anything else. The beginning, the first move, fresh start, starting point, the place of new departure, a new day.

A. To seek first is to place God on the highest place. (Eph 3:17; Mk 12:30)

- The word dwell comes from two words in the Greek. On means "to live in a home" and the other means "down". Paul prays that our Lord might live in our hearts as His home, that He might feel at home in our hearts. "That Christ may finally settle down and feel comfortably at home in your hearts."

B. To seek first is to have an appetite for spiritual things. (I Cor 2:14-16; 3:1-3)

C. To seek first is to follow God wholeheartedly. (Joshua 14:6-14)

- Three times the words "wholly followed" are used to describe a person who had put God first in his life. At the age of 85, Caleb was still spiritually alert, committed, ready for the challenge. He lived for God wholeheartedly with nothing held back. What kind of an old man do you want to be?

D. To seek first is to commune with God first. (I Chr 28:9; Is 40:31)

- Devotion belongs to the inner life and lives in the closet. It belongs to the person whose thoughts and feelings are devoted to God and who possesses a strong affection for God. This is the genesis of the whole matter of activity and strength of the most energetic, exhaustless and untiring nature. All this is the result of waiting on God.

E. To seek first is to follow and honor Jesus in everything I do. (Phil 1:20-21; Mk 11:29-30)

- Thomas Kempis (a German mystic): "But whoever would fully and feelingly understand the words of Christ must endeavor to conform his life wholly to the life of Christ."

- "What Would Jesus Do" bracelets, the book "In His Steps."

F. To seek first is to remove all the clutter in my life. (Rom 12:1-2)

- Aiden Wilson Tozer (1897-1963): A country boy who, without formal education, became one of the greatest American pastors and leader of Southside Alliance Church in Chicago from 1928 – 1959. As pastor, he did virtually no administrative work or pastoral counseling. He spent his time in prayer, meditation and the word. His books are many.

- Prayer by A.W. Tozer: "Father, I want to know thee, but my coward heart fears to give up its toys. I cannot part with them without inward bleeding, and I do not try to hide from Thee the terror of the parting. I come trembling, but I do come. Please root from my heart all those things which I have cherished so long and which have become a very part of my living self, so that Thou mayest enter and dwell there without a rival. Then shalt Thou make the place of Thy feet glorious. Then shall my heart have no need of the sun to shine in it, for Thyself wilt be the light of it, and there shall be no night there. In Jesus' name, Amen."

- Clutter of unnecessary activities, things, habits, attitudes.

G. To seek first is to be ambitious for God's purposes, setting self aside. (Acts 20:24)

- William Booth, co-founder of the Salvation Army: "One of his biographers tells of the day when the general was in his eighties. He was ill and had been to see a physician. It was left to his son, Bramwell, to tell him that he would soon be blind. "You mean that I am going blind?" "Well, General, I fear that we must contemplate that," said Bramwell, who along with the family had always addressed their father by that affectionate name. There was a pause while Booth thought over what he had been told. And then the father asked the son, "I shall never see your face again?" "No, probably not in this world," was the son's reply. The biographer writes, "During the next few moments the veteran's hand crept along the counterpane to take hold of his son's, and holding it he said very calmly, 'God must know best!' And after another pause, 'Bramwell, I have done what I could for God and for the people with my eyes. Now I shall do what I can for God and for the people without my eyes.'"

SAMPLE SERMON OUTLINE

H. To seek first is to give God the priority that is His due. (Phil 3:13-14)

I. To seek first is to seek first His rule, His will and His authority. (Col. 1:13-14)

J.   To seek first is to be in complete submission to
     the Holy Spirit in both decisions and behavior.
     (Ezek. 36:26-27; John 14:15-16; Eph. 5:18-19;
     Gal. 5:25)

K.   To seek first is to have a heart sensitive to sin
     and anything that offends God. (Eph. 4:30)

[1] Charles R. Swindoll. *The Tale of the Tardy Oxcart* (Nashville:
Word Publishing, 1998), p. 308.

[2] Gordon MacDonald. *The Life God Blesses* (Nashville: Thomas
Nelson Publishers, 1994), pp. 65-66.

Appendix B: A Foundational Research Library for Preachers

Greek Research Tools

- *New Strong's Exhaustive Concordance* by James Strong (Thomas Nelson/Word, 2000)

- *The New Englishman's Greek Concordance* by George V. Wigram (Hendrickson Publishers, 1996)

- *The New Greek English Lexicon of the New Testament* by Joseph Thayer (Hendrickson Publishers, 1996)

- *New International Dictionary of New Testament Theology,* 4 volumes by Colin Brown (Zondervan, 1986)

- *Word Pictures in the New Testament* by A.T. Robertson (Broadman/Holman)

- *The Word Study New Testament and Concordance,* 2 volumes by Ralph Winter (Tyndale House, 1978)

- *Vincent's New Testament Word Studies,* 4 volumes by Marvin Vincent (Hendrickson Publishers, 1986)

- *Word Meanings in the New Testament* by Ralph Earle (Hendrickson Publishers, 1986)

- *New Testament Words* by William Barclay (Westminster/John Knox, 1974)

- *Theological Dictionary of the New Testament* by Gerhard Kittel (Eerdmans Publishing, 1964 for the 10 volume set or 1985 for one volume set)

- *Vine's Complete Expository Dictionary of Old and New Testament Words* by W.E. Vine (Thomas Nelson/ Word, 1985)

Hebrew Research Tools

- ❧ *The Englishman's Hebrew Concordance of the Old Testament* by George V. Wigram (Hendrickson Publishers, 1996)

- ❧ *Gesenius' Hebrew-Chaldee Lexicon* to the Old Testament by H.W.F. Gesenius (Baker/Revell, 1979)

- ❧ *Theological Wordbook of the Old Testament,* 2 volumes edited by R.L. Harris, G.L. Archer, Jr. and B.K. Waltke (Moody Press, 1980)

- ❧ *Wilson's Old Testament Word Studies* by William Wilson (Hendrickson Publishers)

Commentaries

- *Lenski New Testament Commentaries,* 12 volumes by R.C.H. Lenski (Hendrickson Publishers, 1942)

- *Barnes Notes on the Old and New Testaments* by Albert Barnes (Baker/Revell)

- *Explore the Book,* J. Sidlow Baxter (Zondervan Publishing)

- *Keil & Delitzsch Old Testament Commentary on the Old Testament,* 10 volumes by C.F. Keil (Hendrickson Publishers, 2001)

- *Expositions of the Holy Scriptures* by MacLaren (Baker Publishing), 17 volumes.

- *The Preacher's Homiletic Commentary,* 31 volumes (Baker Publishing)

Appendix C: Scriptures on Preaching

Isaiah 61:1

> The Spirit of the Lord God is upon Me, because the Lord has anointed Me to preach good tidings to the poor; He has sent Me to heal the brokenhearted, to proclaim liberty to the captives, and the opening of the prison to those who are bound.

Amos 8:11

> "Behold, the days are coming," says the Lord God, "That I will send a famine on the land, not a famine of bread, nor a thirst for water, but of hearing the words of the Lord."

2 Timothy 4:2

> Preach the word! Be ready in season and out of season. Convince, rebuke, exhort, with all long-suffering and teaching.

Titus 2:1

> But as for you, speak the things which are proper for sound doctrine.

Luke 16:16

> The law and the prophets were until John. Since that time the kingdom of God has been preached, and everyone is pressing into it.

2 Peter 2:5

> And did not spare the ancient world, but saved Noah, one of eight people, a preacher of righteousness, bringing in the flood on the world of the ungodly.

Matthew 3:1

> In those days John the Baptist came preaching in the wilderness of Judea.

Matthew 4:17

> From that time Jesus began to preach and to say, "Repent, for the kingdom of heaven is at hand."

Matthew 10:7

> And as you go preach, saying, The kingdom of heaven is at hand.

Matthew 24:14

> And this gospel of the kingdom will be preached in all the world as a witness to all the nations, and then the end will come.

Titus 1:3

> But has in due time manifested His word through preaching, which was committed to me according to the commandment of God our Savior.

Acts 6:4

> But we will give ourselves continually to prayer and to the ministry of the word.

Colossians 1:28

> Him we preach, warning every man and teaching every man in all wisdom, that we may present every man perfect in Christ Jesus.

Haggai 1:13

> Then Haggai, the Lord's messenger, spoke the Lord's message to the people, saying, "I am with you, says the Lord."

Mark 16:15

> And He said to them, Go into all the world and preach the gospel to every creature.

1 Corinthians 9:16

> For if I preach the gospel, I have nothing to boast of, for necessity is laid upon me; yes, woe is me if I do not preach the gospel!

2 Corinthians 4:5

> For we do not preach ourselves, but Christ Jesus the Lord, and ourselves your bondservants for Jesus' sake.

2 Timothy 2:15

Be diligent to present yourself approved to God, a worker who does not need to be ashamed, rightly dividing the word of truth.

2 Timothy 3:16

All Scripture is given by inspiration of God, and is profitable for doctrine, for reproof, for correction, for instruction in righteousness.

Appendix D: Preachers on Preaching

❧ *Richard Cecil:* "To love to preach is one thing. To love those to whom we preach quite another."

❧ *Jay Adams:* "The preacher is there to deliver the message of God, a message from God to the people, a mouthpiece of God. He is there to do something to the people, produce results, influence people. It should change the person listening in every way—emotionally, mentally, directionally, spiritually."

❧ *Samuel Rutherford:* "I preached as never sure to preach again, and as a dying man to dying men." [also attributed to others]

❧ *Origen* (A.D. 180-253): "I do not disdain rhetoric itself, but rather the misuse of it. Regarding style, but a lucid discourse, the splendor of eloquence and the art of arguing with propriety are admitted to the service of the word of God."

❧ *Joseph Parker:* "The preacher is not an author reading his own manuscript. He is a voice, a fire, a herald, bold and eager in his sacred work, an orator speaking in heaven's name and strength."

❧ *John Stott:* "The systematic preaching of the word is impossible without the systematic studying of it. We must daily soak ourselves in the scriptures."

❧ *Martin Luther:* "Prayer, meditation and suffering make a preacher. The stars shine the brightest when the night is the darkest and God is able to give us songs in the night."

❧ *George A. Buttrick:* "Preaching is, in one regard, like bringing up children. We know all about it until we have to do it, then we know nothing."

❧ *Fredrick Buechner:* "Often, I'm afraid, the church is a place where preachers preach, not out of their depths, but out of their shallows."

Appendix E: Internet Resources for Preachers

Links to additional Christian websites are listed on many of the sites below.

- ❧ www.AllAboutGod.com

- ❧ www.AmazingBible.com

- ❧ www.Bible.org

- ❧ www.BibleFacts.org

- ❧ www.BibleGateway.com

- ❧ www.Bible-HQ.com

- ❧ www.BlueLetterBible.org

- ❧ www.CARM.org (Christian Apologetics)

- www.Christian-thinktank.com

- www.ChristianWebSite.com

- www.Crosswalk.com

- www.GotQuestions.org

- www.Gospelcom.net

- www.ICLnet.org (Internet Christian Library)

- www.Pastors.com

- www.SeekFind.org

- www.SermonSearch.com

- www.SermonIllustrations.com

- www.StudyLight.org

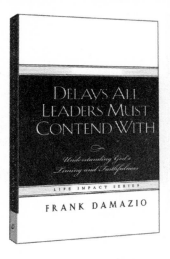

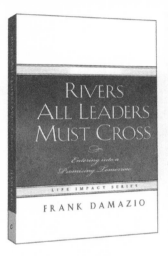

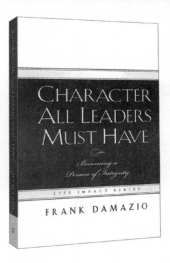

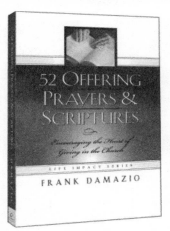

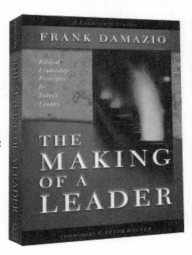

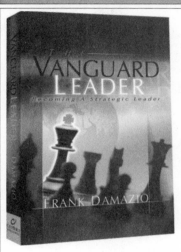

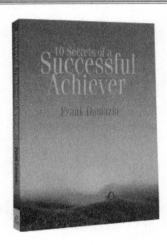

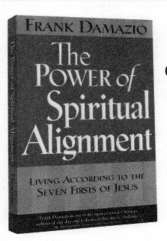